D0753536

# From HEAD to TAIL

## All About HORSE CARE

by Donna Bowman Bratton

Consultant:
Jennifer A. Zablotny, DVM
American Veterinary Medical Association
Michigan Veterinary Medical Association

CAPSTONE PRESS
a capstone imprint

Snap Books are published by Capstone Press,
1710 Roe Crest Drive, North Mankato, Minnesota 56003
www.capstonepub.com

**Library of Congress Cataloging-in-Publication Data**
Bratton, Donna Bowman, author.
From head to tail : all about horse care / by Donna
Bowman Bratton.
pages cm. — (Snap books. Crazy about horses)
Summary: "Photos and text introduce readers to horse
care, including general information about how to
maintain a horse, habitat, diet, and grooming needs
and equipment"— Provided by publisher.
Audience: Ages 8–14.
Audience: Grades 4 to 6.
Includes bibliographical references and index.
ISBN 978-1-4914-0709-7 (library binding)
ISBN 978-1-4914-0715-8 (eBook PDF)
1. Horses—Juvenile literature. 2. Horses—Health—Juvenile
literature. I. Title.
SF951.B83 2015
636.108'3—dc23                                    2014006651

**Editorial Credits**
Michelle Hasselius, editor; Kazuko Collins and
Juliette Peters, designers; Deirdre Barton, media
researcher; Laura Manthe, production specialist

**Photo Credits**
Capstone Studio: Karon Dubke, 9(top); CLiX Photography:
Shawn Hamilton,  5(bottom), 15(t), 21(b); Shutterstock:
Anastasila Golovkova, horse silhouette, Anastasija Popova,
17(b), 29(top left), andersphoto, tooled leather design
element, AZP Worldwide, 10, Banana Republic Images,
31, bepsy, 12, Clara, 23, eastern light photography, 4, 11(t),
22, Eric Isselee, 27(t), Gail Johnson, 16, Gary C. Tognoni,
32, Goldika, 28 (top right), Hamik, 7, ILiyan, 8, Johnny
Adolphson, 28(tl), Joy Brown, 19, joyful, 29(tr), jurraB, 18,
Karen Givens, 20(b), Makarova Viktoria, cover, 2-3, mariait,
14, MaxyM, 26, melis, 25(t), Miao Liao, 6, Moriz, 5(t), Nate
Allred, 11(b), nuttakit, leather strip design element, Pawell
Kazmierczak, 29(b), Raymond B. Summers, 13(t), Reinhold
Leitner, wood design element, Rita Kochmarjova, 17(t),
24, Robert Hoetink, 15(b), Stephanie Coffman, 9(b), thinz,
stripe, flower design elements, Thitisan krobkham, 28(b),
tomashko, 25(b), TTstudio, 20(t), Volker Rauch, 21(tr), VVO,
27(b), Zuzule, 1, 13(b); Wikipedia: BLW, 21(tl)

Glossary terms are bolded on first use in text.

Printed in the United States of America in North Mankato, Minnesota.
032014      008087CGF14

# TABLE of CONTENTS

# Our LARGEST Pets

Are you crazy about horses? You're not alone. People have had a special relationship with horses for centuries. Ancestors of today's horses date back 55 million years, to a horse that was the size of a fox. It had four toes on its front feet and three toes on its back feet.

It took millions of years for horses to become the graceful animals known today. There are an estimated 58 million horses in the world, and most of them are pets. That's a lot of horses for girls to love. Learning to take care of these large pets is a big responsibility.

# A HORSE IS A HORSE

Here are some things all horses have in common.

mane

withers

tail

muzzle

hoof

## DID YOU KNOW?

Before tape measures, people measured a horse's height by counting hand-widths from the ground to the horse's withers. Today a horse's height is still measured in hands. One hand equals 4 inches (10 centimeters).

5

# HOME for a HORSE

The ideal home for a horse is in a safe **pasture** with other horses. This open, grassy area should have strong fences and gates. Fences and gates should be made from materials that are safe for horses. Barbed wire should never be used. The sharp barbs on the wire fencing can cause serious injuries. Pastures should have lots of healthy grass. There also needs to be a shelter to protect against bad weather. Trees can shade a horse from the summer sun, but they can't protect against wind, rain, snow, and hail. For horses that aren't kept in stables, a three-sided shed that faces away from the worst winds is ideal.

## A SAFE SPACE

Horse owners should inspect the area before their horses move in. They should remove things like trash, nails, soda cans, broken glass, and loose wire. If a horse eats poisonous weeds, it can become very sick. These should also be removed.

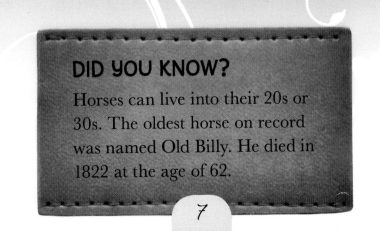

### DID YOU KNOW?

Horses can live into their 20s or 30s. The oldest horse on record was named Old Billy. He died in 1822 at the age of 62.

Boarding stables rent space for horses. Many stable owners agree to feed these horses when owners can't. In herds horses always stick together in small groups. So it's best to look for a stable that boards several horses.

Stables should be well built with plenty of **ventilation** for clean air and good **drainage** to keep floors dry. Check for sharp edges or nails that could hurt the horse. Make sure the horse has at least a 12-by-12-foot (3.6-by-3.6-meter) **stall**, to allow plenty of space to move around. Safe bedding for the floor keeps horses comfortable and dry. Wood shavings, straw, and rubber mats are good options.

# HORSE CARE IS A DIRTY JOB

A horse can produce up to 50 pounds (23 kilograms) of manure every day. So it's important to clean, or **muck**, horse stalls daily. Horse owners should keep a stall fork, shovel, wheelbarrow, and broom handy. They should wear boots and an old pair of jeans for the dirtiest work of horse care.

## DID YOU KNOW?

Many stables have outdoor runs attached to stalls. These runs are like tiny yards.

# HUNGRY *Horses*

Horses are built to **graze** on grass all day and night. This constant walking to find food gives them lots of exercise. You might say horses are munching athletes.

Hay is the next best thing to grass, but sometimes horses need grain too. Grain is a good option for stabled horses that don't have access to grass. Grain also can provide extra nutrition for older horses and extra calories for work and show horses.

The climate, a horse's age, weight, and activity level will help determine the amount and type of food it needs. There are many kinds of horse feed available. Horse owners should ask a veterinarian or horse care expert about the best diet for their horses.

## DID YOU KNOW?

The average 1,000-pound (454-kg) horse eats about 25 pounds (11 kg) of food a day. Most of that should come from grass or hay.

Owners of older horses may need to soak food in water first. This softens the food, making it easier for older horses to eat.

## A SWEET TREAT

Occasionally it's OK for horses to have a special treat. Stick to natural foods like apples or carrots. But remember too many treats can upset a horse's stomach.

### Sticky Horse Treats

Coat a carrot or half an apple in corn syrup. Cover with dry oats to make a healthy horse snack.

# GULP, GULP, GULP

Horses need lots of water to stay healthy. You'd be thirsty too if you ate that much dry food. Horses can drink up to 20 gallons (76 liters) of water every day. Ponds, lakes, or other natural water sources usually provide safe drinking water for horses. If **water troughs** or buckets are used, it is important to keep them clean and full of fresh water to avoid **bacteria**.

## WINTER WOES

On cold winter days, it's nice to be warm and cozy inside. But horse owners can't get too comfy. They must care for their horses in all types of weather. Here are some winter tips to keep horses safe.

* Check water buckets and troughs several times a day to be sure the horse's water hasn't frozen. Consider using heated buckets and water troughs.
* Ask a veterinarian about increasing hay or grain during winter months. A horse may need the extra calories to stay warm.
* Provide shelter from the wind, rain, and snow.
* A horse's fuzzy winter coat may not be enough to keep it warm when it's cold out. A horse blanket might be necessary.
* Don't stop spending time with a horse just because it's cold. A horse needs attention and exercise during the winter too.

### DID YOU KNOW?

Daylight controls when a horse grows its fuzzy winter coat. Shorter fall and winter days work like a natural timer, signaling a wardrobe change to a thicker coat.

# EXERCISE

Imagine being cooped up in your bedroom all day and night. You would go stir crazy. A horse doesn't want to be stuck in a stall all day either. Horses are built to move. They need 30 to 60 minutes of exercise most days of the week.

Most horses need free time in a pasture or arena. They can kick up their heels, run, and wander freely. It is the ultimate recess time. When a horse is cooped up in a stall, keep it entertained with special horse toys like giant balls and knotted ropes. Some racehorses and show horses even go swimming in special pools or use horse-sized treadmills to stay in shape.

## LONGE LINE

Using a longe line lets a horse get exercise in a controlled environment. The horse is attached to a 20- to 30-foot (6.1- to 9.1-m) longe line that the owner holds. The horse moves in a wide circle around its owner. A horse can learn to longe by making small circles during walks. With a little practice, the horse can learn to change speed with different vocal commands.

### DID YOU KNOW?

In the wild, horses can walk up to 50 miles (80 kilometers) a day.

# GET BACK *in the* SADDLE

Horse riding is great exercise for the horse and rider. It's also a fun way to learn and explore areas together. Riders can go on trails or through large fields. They can also get involved in horse shows. Whether riding for fun or training for a horse show, young riders should have adult supervision at all times.

# BEWARE OF THE KICK!

In the wild good eyesight helps horses detect **predators**. Horses can see almost directly behind them. If they are startled or feel threatened, horses can send a powerful kick. Stay safe and never sneak up behind a horse.

canter

## DID YOU KNOW?

Horses move by using four different gaits—walk, trot, canter, and gallop.

# HORSE Grooming

Grooming a horse is a good way to create a special bond while keeping the horse looking great. Before reaching for a saddle, a rider should always groom his or her horse to make sure dirt and burrs aren't rubbing against it. Grooming is the perfect time to check for health concerns too. In herds horses regularly groom each other with their teeth. Thankfully people just need some basic tools.

## Coat Brushes

Unlike your hair, a horse's coat doesn't need to be brushed every day unless it's really messy. But most horses like being brushed. There are stiff-bristled brushes, used for thicker coats or when there's lots of dirt. There are also soft bristle brushes for polishing shorter coats. A rubber curry comb can remove dried mud and loose hair. Rubbing the curry in a circular motion feels like a massage to a horse.

### DID YOU KNOW?

A dirty horse can be a good thing. That dirt is natural protection against sun, water, and insects.

## Manes and Tails

Long, short, curly, straight—there are all kinds of manes and tails. While grooming a horse, don't forget to tackle tangles and burrs. A wide-toothed comb or stiff brush will do the trick. Tangle-free tails are important because they act as a horse's built-in fly swatter.

## Bathing

Many horses like to be rinsed off in hot weather, but they rarely need soapy baths. When preparing for summertime competitions, riders may decide to break out the horse shampoo. Give the horse a chance to get used to the water by getting its legs wet first. A horse doesn't like to get its head wet, so use a damp sponge to wash that adorable face.

There are different mane and tail style options for horse competitions.

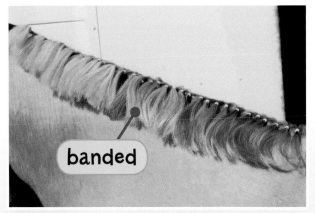

**banded**—tiny ponytails in the mane that lay flat against the neck

**plaited**—braiding or weaving designs in a horse's mane

**plaited tail**—the hair is French braided and goes three-fourths of the way down the tailbone

**roached**—manes that are shaved to look like a man's crew cut

**banged**—the end of a long tail is trimmed straight across

## DID YOU KNOW?

Braiding a horse's tail when it's wet can create a wavy look after it dries.

# HEALTHY *Hooves*

FROG

Horses can't survive without four hooves to support their weight. Hooves are made of layers of thick protein called keratin, just like your fingernails. In the middle of the hoof, there is a triangle-shaped cushion under the heel called a frog. The frog is especially sensitive to stones and hard dirt. A **hoof pick** is used to safely clean hooves from heel to toe.

When your fingernails get too long, you can trim them with nail clippers and a file. Every six weeks a horse's hooves need to be trimmed by a farrier. These professionals care for hooves. Farriers will keep hooves the right length to prevent cracking. They use hoof-sized clippers called nippers. Farriers also use large nail files called rasps. If a horse needs horseshoes, the farrier knows how to shape and attach them properly. One set of shoes should last a horse for six weeks.

## DID YOU KNOW?

Show horses can wear clear or black hoof polish for special events.

# Pearly WHITES

Losing a baby tooth is a big deal. Horses have baby teeth too. It takes about 4.5 years for a horse to lose its last baby tooth. By then it has 36 to 44 permanent teeth. But those teeth continue to grow throughout a horse's life. In the wild, grazing helps a horse's teeth stay smooth and healthy. But a **domestic** horse's diet isn't the same as a wild horse. Sometimes its upper and lower teeth can rub against each other, filing them into sharp points that look like fangs. Imagine not being able to eat because sharp teeth cut into your cheeks, gums, or tongue. Ouch!

Not eating can lead to **malnutrition**. This is especially a problem with older horses. An equine dentist can file down sharp points with a dental rasp. They watch for other mouth problems too. Equine dentists are veterinarians who receive special training to take care of a horse's teeth. It's a good idea for a horse to get a dental checkup at least once a year.

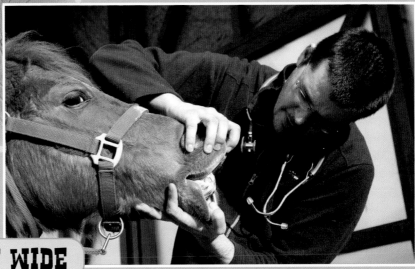

## OPEN WIDE

You can't ask a horse to climb into a dentist's chair and open wide. Usually the dentist will give the horse medicine to help it relax for the exam. A special brace called a speculum keeps its mouth open while the dentist works. Many of their tools are just like the ones your dentist uses—only larger. Dentists look for gum disease, decay, and broken or loose teeth. They also check the horse's ability to chew. After a dental appointment, a horse needs a break from riding for a day or two.

### DID YOU KNOW?

Professionals can estimate a horse's age by the amount of wear on its teeth.

# HORSE *Health*

Keeping this four-legged friend healthy as a horse requires constant care and regular checkups with a veterinarian. A veterinarian can give horses their required **vaccinations** and teach owners how to treat for **parasites**.

But getting a horse to a vet can be a big challenge. Many horse vets will come right to the barn or stable. Their trucks are stocked like an animal clinic on wheels.

# WHEN TO CALL A VETERINARIAN

Horses can't tell you when they're feeling sick, so how do owners know when to call the vet? Sometimes, it's as easy as ABC.

Appearance—Does the horse look like its normal self? Does it have a runny nose, an open wound, or a new limp?

Behavior—How is the horse acting? Is it grouchy or sleepy? Is it eating and drinking well?

Condition—Are there any changes in the horse's weight or to its coat?

# STABLE FIRST-AID

Every stable and horse owner should have a first-aid kit. They can be purchased, or people can make a basic kit themselves. Some things that should be included are:

- ❏ phone numbers of at least two veterinarians
- ❏ small flashlight
- ❏ hand sanitizer
- ❏ detergent; dish soap will work
- ❏ non-latex gloves
- ❏ petroleum jelly
- ❏ scissors
- ❏ bandages of different sizes
- ❏ antibiotic ointment
- ❏ leg wraps
- ❏ rolled cotton
- ❏ hydrogen peroxide
- ❏ rubbing alcohol
- ❏ large-dose syringe

# TEST YOUR HORSE CARE IQ

1. A horse's favorite home would be _____?
   a. a small stall
   b. a safe pasture with a shelter
   c. your backyard

2. The amount and type of feed a horse needs depends on _____.
   a. the horse's age, weight, and activity level
   b. how hungry it is
   c. which brand costs less

3. How much water does a horse drink every day?
   a. one cup (.2 L)
   b. 12 to 20 gallons (45 to 76 L)
   c. 10,000 gallons (38,000 L)

4. What kind of fencing should be avoided?
   a. barbed wire
   b. pole fencing
   c. wood fencing

5. How often should a horse's hooves be trimmed?

a. once a week
b. every six weeks
c. once a year

6. A vet should be called if there is a change in a horse's _____.

a. appearance
b. behavior
c. condition
d. all of the above

# GLOSSARY

**bacteria** (bak-TEER-ee-uh)—one-celled, tiny living things; some are helpful and some cause disease

**domestic** (duh-MES-tik)—no longer wild

**drainage** (DRAY-nij)—a way to get rid of extra water

**graze** (GRAYZ)—to eat grass and other plants

**hoof pick** (HOOF pik)—a curved, pointy tool used to remove stones and dirt from hooves

**malnutrition** (mal-noo-TRISH-uhn)—a serious condition caused by a lack of healthy foods

**muck** (MUHK)—to remove manure or dirt from an animal's stall

**parasite** (PAIR-uh-site)—something that lives on or inside an animal or plant and causes harm

**pasture** (PASS-chur)—open land where animals eat grass and exercise

**predator** (PRED-uh-tur)—an animal that hunts other animals for food

**stall** (STAHL)—a small area in a stable or barn where an animal is kept

**vaccination** (vak-suh-NAY-shun)—a shot of medicine that protects animals from a disease

**ventilation** (ven-tuh-LAY-shuhn)—a system or means of providing fresh air

**water trough** (WAW-tur trawf)—a long, narrow container that holds water for animals

# READ MORE

**Niven, Felicia Lowenstein.** *Learning to Care for a Horse.* Beginning Pet Care with American Humane. Berkeley Heights, N.J.: Bailey Books/Enslow, 2011.

**Sexton, Colleen.** *Caring for Your Horse.* Blastoff! Readers. Pet Care Library. Minneapolis: Bellwether Media, 2010.

**Young, Rae.** *Drawing Arabians and Other Amazing Horses.* Drawing Horses. North Mankato, Minn.: Capstone Press, 2014.

# INTERNET SITES

FactHound offers a safe, fun way to find Internet sites related to this book. All of the sites on FactHound have been researched by our staff.

Here's all you do:

Visit *www.facthound.com*

Type in this code: 9781491407097

Super-cool stuff! Check out projects, games and lots more at **www.capstonekids.com**

# INDEX